leap THROUGH TIME

Castle

First published in 2001 by Orpheus Books Ltd, 2 Church Green,
Witney, Oxon OX28 4AW

Created and produced by Nicholas Harris and Claire Aston,
Orpheus Books Ltd

Text Nicholas Harris

Illustrator Peter Dennis *(Linda Rogers Associates)*

Consultant Richard Platt

Printed and bound in Singapore

leap THROUGH TIME

Castle

illustrated by

Peter Dennis

orpheus

Contents

Introduction

Imagine you are standing on a hilltop somewhere in Europe, thousands of years ago. Some farming people have gathered to make their home here. They have built simple shelters and a high fence all around their camp to protect it. As the years go by, other people come to live on the same hilltop. They put up stronger and stronger defences, finally building a castle with thick stone walls. The new castle will live a long and eventful life ...

The story told in this book is like a journey. It is not a journey you can make by plane, car or ship. In fact, you don't have to go anywhere at all. You are about to travel through time. With each turn of the page, the date moves forward a few days, years or centuries. You are still in the same place, but notice how many things change from one date to the next. Each date—each stop on your journey—is like a new chapter. The early forts, the building of the stone castle, the preparations to defend it, the siege, the rebuilding and fall to ruin—all tell the story of the castle.

Look out for a pair of lovers. They appear in every illustration, although sometimes they are quite hard to find!

Use this thumb index to travel though time! Just find the page you want to see and flip it open. This way you can make a quick comparison between one scene and another, even though some show events that took place many years apart. A little black arrow on the page points to the time of the scene illustrated on that page.

The year 600 BC

Some farming people decide to build their village on a hilltop. The villagers' houses are round and made mostly of wood. Each has a cone-shaped framework of branches held up by posts driven into the ground. Bundles of reeds (a thatch) form a roof, while dried mud or stone makes up the outside walls.

To protect their village, the people build up "walls" of earth called ramparts all round it. On top of the ramparts they erect wooden

The entrance to the village, the gateway, is the most strongly defended part of all. Any attackers would have to climb the ramparts, cross the ditches—then face guards hurling spears down at them from behind palisades.

Ditch

Building under construction

Gateway

Ramparts

fences called palisades. Safe inside the hillfort, the villagers tend their animals, cook food, chop wood, grind corn and weave cloth.

THE CELTS

The Celts, the first people to build a "castle" on this hilltop site, were a farming people from central Europe. Over the years they spread across Europe. They were divided into many separate tribes and often fought one another for land. Besides being farmers, they were skilled metalworkers and active traders. As warriors, they were no match for the powerful Roman armies, who began to conquer most of their lands after 225 BC.

Grain store

Palisade

Ramparts

Thatched roof

Cooking

Chariot

Pigs

Weaving

The year AD 100

Ditch

Gateway

Toilet block

Barracks

Soldiers

Soldiers' quarters

Principia

Chapel

Courtyard

Stable

The Celts' hillfort was no defence against the mighty Romans. A Roman legion (group of soldiers) has quickly conquered the fort and built a new fort in its place. It has strong defences, with ramparts built up from layers of turf on the inside and stone walls on the outside. For a neat finish, the walls are plastered, with a brickwork pattern painted in red.

Inside the Roman fort are the soldiers' barracks. Their commander lives in a separate, much grander stone building. It has heated rooms and plenty of space for his family and servants. The fort's head-quarters is called the principia. A statue of the emperor is kept there. It is under guard at all times.

Gateway

Section of wall cut away

Bedroom

Commanding officer's house

Ramparts

Stone walls

Dining room

Courtyard

Kitchen

Entrance hall

Waiting room

Food store

Stable yard

A thousand years later ...

The old Roman fort that once stood on top of this hill was deserted many centuries ago. People used the stone for building their own houses.

Now the Normans have arrived. The hilltop site is a perfect place for a new fort from which to rule over their lands. A Norman lord orders local people to build a large mound of earth called a "motte". A wooden tower is built on the mound, surrounded by a high palisade. At the base of the motte is a courtyard, or bailey, where there is a hall, chapel, barn, stables and other buildings. The bailey is also surrounded by a palisade and a ditch.

All the buildings are made of wood. They would easily be destroyed by fire, so the Normans plan to replace the fort with a stone castle one day.

The entrance to the castle is by drawbridge. If danger threatened, it would be quickly hauled up. But should the attackers gain entry, the defenders would hurry up to the motte, demolishing the stairway behind them.

Hall

Stables

Gate

Drawbridge

Tower

Plastered palisade

Motte

Bailey

Grain store

Well

Chapel

Hay

Palisade

Ditch

FROM ROMANS TO NORMANS

The Romans' great empire lasted for many years, but it eventually collapsed in the late 5th century AD. Germanic peoples from the east, whom the Romans called "barbarians", invaded the western Roman empire. They settled in their new lands and set up their own kingdoms. One group, the Franks, ruled over the most powerful kingdom.

Another barbarian people invaded western Europe in the late 700s. These were the Vikings, who came from Denmark, Sweden and Norway. Many settled in the lands they invaded, including Britain and France. The Normans, descendants of the Vikings, were a powerful people from Northern France.

Thirty years later ...

The hilltop site has been chosen by a powerful lord to be the place where his new fortress home is to be built. The lord must have a strong, stone-built castle from which to rule over his surrounding lands.

About 1000 men work on building the new castle. A master mason is in charge of the building work. He has a team of masons under him. Some (freemasons) cut and carve the stone while others (roughmasons) build the walls. Carpenters make the wooden frame for the roof and build the scaffolding, wooden planks fixed to the walls that allow men to work high up on the new castle's walls. Blacksmiths make and repair tools.

Besides the craftsmen there are the labourers, workers who carry heavy loads and winch stones and timbers up to the top of the castle. A treadwheel is a machine that helps with this task. As a man walks inside it, it turns, pulling on a thick rope with pincers on the end of it.

The thick castle walls are not made of solid stone. In between the outer layers of smooth, carved stone is a mass of rubble.

Master mason

Treadwheel

Scaffolding

Outer
(curtain)
wall

Rubble
inside wall

Carpenter

Lead
roof

Treadwheel

Hoist

Keep

Limewashing
the walls

13

MIDDLE AGES
This period in history is known as the Middle Ages. In those days, the king gave land to his nobles (barons or lords) in return for their support in ruling the country. Noble families became powerful.

Keep

Bakery

Lord and lady

Pigsty

Stores

Well

Ten years later...

At last, the castle is complete. The magnificent stone keep, gleaming white in the sun, towers above the cottages gathered inside the walls. Delighted with their new home, the lord and lady set off on horseback for a day's falconry, accompanied by their favourite dogs.

Meanwhile, the castle is buzzing with activity. The steward checks the food store, fresh water is drawn from the well and workers are hard at work in the kitchens preparing the meal for when the lord returns. A blacksmith makes shoes for one of the lord's horses. Up on the battlements, the guards keep watch.

600 BC

AD 100

1000 years later

30 years later

10 years later

Battlements

Blacksmith's forge

Kitchen

Hayloft

Stables

15

In the Middle Ages, falcons, kinds of birds of prey, were used as hunting animals. A falconer would wear a gauntlet to protect his hand, and carry a leash to prevent the birds from flying away.

Falconer

Taster

Lady

Lord

Cup-bearer

Steward (castle manager)

High table

Carver

Washing hands before meal

Floor strewn with sweet-scented herbs

A hundred years later...

We are in the great hall. A grand banquet is in full swing in honour of the lord's guest, a neighbouring baron. The two men have made an alliance, an agreement to help defend each other's lands in the event of war. It is time to celebrate!

The servants bring in the dishes. The first to be served are the lord and lady and their guests. They sit at the top table, which is covered with a linen tablecloth. They eat off gold and silver plates and drink from individual cups. The meat is carved at the lord's table and the best pieces are served to him and his honoured guests.

The other diners sit at trestle tables. Their food is served up on dishes called messes. Each mess is shared between three or four people. They eat not from plates but from trenchers, slices of stale bread that soak up the gravy (afterwards they will be given to the poor to eat). They share their drinks from jugs. Table manners are important—although not everyone cares about them!

Musicians in gallery

Entertainers

17

Most castles had spiral staircases (you can see one being built on page 12). They usually spiralled upwards in a clockwise direction. This gave the advantage to the castle's defenders (provided they were right-handed) because it was easier for a swordsman to strike at an opponent standing lower on the stairs, who had to lean round the corner to use *his* sword.

A few weeks later...

The guards are in a hurry to prepare the castle's defences. Another baron has found out that two of his rivals have formed an alliance. News has come that he means to destroy the castle.

The castle has impressive defences. A deep ditch and a high wall several metres thick run all round it. The castle gateway is especially strong. A drawbridge that crosses the ditch could be quickly raised up to block the entrance. Behind it are heavy gates and two portcullises, heavy gratings that slide down grooves in the walls. Defenders could shoot arrows or drop stones down through "murder holes" on to the heads of attackers.

The castle's defenders build wooden hoardings around the battlements. From these, men could drop missiles on attackers standing close to the walls. Workers stretch damp hides over the hoardings to protect them from fire.

Preparations are nearly complete. Will the castle be strong enough to withstand enemy attack?

Building wooden hoardings

Outer (curtain) wall

Guardroom

Dungeon

Ditch

18

Gatehouse

Drawbridge winch

Portcullis

Murder holes

Gate

Drawbridge

Latrine (toilet)

Damp hides

Gong farmer
(empties latrine pit)

600 BC

AD 100

1000 years later

30 years later

10 years later

100 years later

A few weeks later

Keep

Bailey

Gatehouse

A plan of the castle, showing
the position of the gatehouse.

A crossbowman loads a bolt into his weapon.

One way of breaking down a castle's walls was by undermining. Miners dug a tunnel beneath the walls, removing soil and rocks. The miners set fire to the wooden props that supported it and retreated. The tunnel collapsed, bringing down the walls above it.

Wooden hoardings

Dead animal being slung by trebuchet

Drawbridge

Battering ram

Trebuchet

Ladder

Mangonel

Infilled ditch

A few days later...

Foot soldiers climb on to battlements

Belfry

The siege is under way. The enemy soldiers surround the castle and start to build the weapon machines they need to attack the castle.

The soldiers fill in the ditch with stones and sticks. Now the belfry, a giant tower on wheels, can be rolled up close to the walls. Soldiers race up its ladder and leap over the battlements.

Meanwhile, crossbowmen and archers shoot their bolts and arrows. Catapults pound the walls with missiles or fire flaming objects into the wooden hoardings. The giant trebuchet flings rocks or the bodies of animals (or the heads of executed prisoners) into the castle, while the mangonel lobs small boulders. Other soldiers try to force their way through the gate using a battering ram, a tree trunk swung with great force from inside a wooden frame.

Soon the attacking soldiers force their way in. Fire ravages the building. Eventually the great stone castle will be completely destroyed ...

600 BC

AD 100

1000 years later

30 years later

10 years later

100 years later

A few weeks later

A few days later

A hundred years later...

After the siege, the castle was left in ruins. But it was not long before another lord decided to build a new castle in the same commanding hilltop position.

This castle is quite different to the earlier one. Although it still has thick, high walls and towers, there is no keep.

Knights were the most important fighting men of the Middle Ages. Skilled in combat and horsemanship, they were also expected to be honourable and brave. The first knights wore chain-mail coats, made of thousands of metal rings linked together. By the 1400s, knights had switched to wearing suits of plate armour, which were more protective.

Watchtower

Bedroom

Chapel

Guard

Schoolroom

Brewery

Courtya

22

Knight

All the main buildings are built inside the walls. They are more comfortable than the cramped, draughty keep. The round towers defend the castle. Inside them are extra rooms for guests.

Today, the lord is performing a dubbing ceremony. A young man is to be made a knight. The lord taps him on the shoulder with a sword, followed by a blow with the flat side of the blade.

Battlements

Bedroom

Great Hall

Dubbing ceremony

600 BC

AD 100

1000 years later

30 years later

10 years later

100 years later

A few weeks later

A few days later

100 years later

Two hundred and fifty years later...

This castle is at Saumur, in France. Like many French castles, or *châteaux,* it became a comfortable home for a wealthy family.

This castle was built during the nineteenth century for King Ludwig II of Bavaria, Germany. It was very unusual for a large castle to be built so long after the time of the Middle Ages, but Ludwig was fascinated by the days of knights and castles. He had the wealth to make his dream of a fairytale castle home come true.

Since it was rebuilt, this castle has not suffered any more attacks. The noble family who now live there can enjoy their home in peace. The arrow slits have been replaced by glass windows that let in more light. To the tops of the towers, no longer needed as look-out positions, tall, pointed roofs have been added.

Outer courtyard

Drawbridge

Gatehouse

FROM FORTRESS TO HOME

By the end of the Middle Ages, the power of the noble families had grown weaker. Kings and queens had taken greater control of their kingdoms. Battles between barons were now rare. Castles were, in any case, costly to build and much less useful as means of defence. For example, powerful cannons could blast great holes in the thickest walls. So fewer and fewer nobles built new castles, preferring to live in large houses instead. If a castle had survived undamaged, however, and could be turned into a comfortable home, living in a castle was the height of luxury.

Tower

Stables

Coach house

Outer (curtain) walls

600 BC

AD 100

1000 years later

30 years later

10 years later

100 years later

A few weeks later

A few days later

100 years later

250 years later

25

Even after a castle has crumbled to ruins, many of its original features can still be seen. These are arrow loops, narrow openings in the walls through which arrows were fired. From outside it was difficult to shoot back through them.

Another two hundred and fifty years later...

The castle has fallen to ruin. The noble family that once lived there has moved away. Nobody has come to live in it since. The gardens have become over-grown. Tiles have fallen from the roofs. The weather has damaged the insides of the castle beyond repair. The gleaming white limewash has flaked off the walls. Shrubs start to grow inside rooms left open to the skies.

Industrial town

Outer courtyard

Gatehouse

Drawbridge

Soon, people from nearby villages visit the castle. It has all they need for building or repairing their own homes. They start to chip away at the walls and take away stone, tiles and timbers.

Also visiting the castle are others curious to discover how people lived so many hundreds of years ago. Some find the ruins so fascinating that they decide to paint pictures of them.

Tower

er urtyard

Outer (curtain) walls

600 BC

AD 100

1000 years later

30 years later

10 years later

100 years later

A few weeks later

A few days later

100 years later

250 years later

250 years later

If you look round an old castle, it may be possible to find clues that tell you what the castle was like back in the Middle Ages. Here, for example, is an area of painted plaster. Now faded, it was once covered with bright patterns.

Can you see rows of square holes high up in the walls? These once held joists, long timbers that supported the wooden floors.

You may be able to see fireplaces all over the castle. Open fires were the only way to provide heat to castle rooms. Often, fireplaces can be found high up in the walls. They were once in rooms on higher floors whose floorboards have since disappeared.

Today

The old castle has been undergoing restoration. Its walls have been rebuilt in places, to make sure there is no danger of them falling down. The trees and overgrown vegetation have all been cleared away and replaced by neat lawns and gravelled courtyards. Guard-rails, steps, benches, information boards and kiosks selling guidebooks and souvenirs have all been provided for visitors.

Telescope

Tower

Brewery

School party

Kiosk

Ghost

Information board

People wander around the ruins, admiring the vast walls and towers. Some wonder what life would have been like for castle residents 700 years ago: where the lord and lady slept, what they ate at their banquets or what happened when the castle was besieged. Of course, you have only to turn back through the pages of this book to find these things out for yourself!

CARING FOR RUINS

Many people now think that looking after the ruins of ancient buildings such as castles is very worthwhile. If they were properly cared for, visitors would come to explore them and become interested in what life in a castle was like hundreds of years ago. Many castles all over the world have been carefully restored and opened to the public.

Walkway

Chimney

Joist holes

Great Hall

...er courtyard

600 BC

AD 100

1000 years later

30 years later

10 years later

100 years later

A few weeks later

A few days later

100 years later

250 years later

250 years later

Today

Glossary

Arrow loops Narrow slits in castle walls through which arrows were fired.

Bailey An open area enclosed by the castle walls.

Baron A wealthy nobleman who promised to be loyal to the king. In return, he was given lands.

Battlements The jagged tops of castle walls.

Belfry A tower used by soldiers laying siege to a castle. As tall as the castle battlements, it was wheeled against the walls during an attack.

Curtain wall The outer wall of a castle.

Drawbridge A bridge across a moat or ditch that could be lifted up to prevent entry to a castle.

Gatehouse A tower in the castle walls that contained the entrance to the castle. The gatehouse usually had extra defences.

Hillfort A stronghold built on a hilltop. Its buildings were surrounded by fences, ramparts and ditches.

Hoardings Wooden frames built on to the outside of the battlements. They provided extra protection to the guards on top of the walls during sieges.

Keep The main stone tower inside the castle walls. It housed the living quarters for the castle's residents.

Knight A fighting man who promised loyalty to a baron. He was expected to be honourable and brave.

Legion A body of three to six thousand Roman soldiers.

Limewash A mixture of lime and water used for painting the castle walls. It protected them from rain and made the castle gleam a brilliant white in the sun.

Mangonel A large catapult that fired rocks and missiles at a castle during a siege.

Mason A builder in stone.

Motte A steep mound of earth on top of which a tower was built. A motte-and-bailey was an early type of castle.

Murder holes Holes in the floor above the entrance in the gatehouse. They probably allowed guards to fire arrows or drop missiles on to enemy soldiers below.

Palisades A fence built from wooden stakes used to protect an area or settlement.

Portcullis A heavy wooden grating that could be slid down to close a gateway at the entrance of a castle.

Ramparts Defensive mounds built around an area or settlement.

Siege The surrounding of a castle by an enemy army to prevent supplies from entering it and anyone inside from leaving it.

Trebuchet A giant catapult that hurled missiles such as rocks, dead animals or even human heads into a castle during an attack. It was powered by using heavy weights.

Index